JANE ROSSINGTON'S
The
CROSSROADS
Years

D0305886

The Official Album

WEIDENFELD AND NICOLSON
London

in association with Central Independent Television plc.

ACKNOWLEDGEMENTS

My thanks go to all the cast – and everyone involved in production and behind the scenes – for my happy memories and such a lot of fun over the last twenty-three years.

Thanks are also due to William Smethurst for his advice with this book, and to all who have helped with photographs and recollections.

I am especially indebted to Joanna Toye, one of our scriptwriters, for her invaluable help in selecting the pictures and putting my words together.

Jane Rossington

Copyright © 1988, Central Independent Television plc.

Published in Great Britain by George Weidenfeld & Nicolson Limited
91 Clapham High Street
London SW4 7TA

ISBN 0 297 79270 9

Printed in Great Britain by Jolly & Barber Ltd, Rugby, Warwickshire

Front endpapers:
(left) Meg and Carlos sampling the soup;
(right) David and Barbara Hunter.

Back endpapers:
(left) The Pollard family;
(right) Jill and Adam.

Frontispiece:
David, Sandy, Jill and Meg, 1971.

Contents

Acknowledgements 2

1 In the Beginning 4

   Chef's Special 10

2 Early Days 12

3 Work Hard, Play Hard 18

4 A Way of Life 24

   Famous faces 30

5 The End of the Beginning 32

   Wedding Bells 36

6 The Beginning of the End 40

7 Absent Friends 44

   Romance in the Air 48

8 The Show Goes On 52

9 A New Regime 59

   Moving with the Times 64

10 The Final Chapter 66

1

In the Beginning

'Crossroads Motel, can I help you ?' I can hardly believe it's over twenty-three years since I spoke those words and threw open the doors of the Crossroads Motel to an eager public. It was 4.30 on a foggy November afternoon in 1964, 'Crossroads' was open for business – and I was booked in for just six weeks ! Since then, as Jill, I've had four surnames, a bigamous marriage, two children by different fathers (one of them the result of an affair with my step-brother), a divorce, two miscarriages, a spell of drug addiction and (hardly surprising) a nervous breakdown. And I can honestly say I wouldn't have missed it for the world. . . .

Back in the early sixties, the television screen was positively foaming with soap operas, and every week a new idea would froth from the pen of a would-be writer. Not all of them would wash with the public – who these days remembers 'Swizzlewick' and 'Weavers Green' ? I had a part in one enduring favourite, 'Emergency Ward 10', as Nurse Kate Ford. You could share the gritty everyday life of the North of England in 'Coronation Street' or the glossy saga of life behind the scenes on a magazine in the BBC's 'Compact'. But between London and Weatherfield was a sort of no-man's land – the Midlands.

Reg Watson, the chirpy Australian producer of the popular chat show 'Lunch Box', presented by none other than Noele Gordon, had been badgering the legendary Lew Grade, then head of ATV, to do a soap opera for years. Finally, Lew, wanting to boost viewing figures in the Midlands, agreed – but was still cautious. His initial brief was for a daily serial to run for just 30 episodes – 6 weeks.

They say you can tell a Midlander by the shamrock in his turban, so it was quite a tall order for writers Peter Ling and Hazel Adair, fresh from 'Compact'. They set to work and came up with something called 'The Midland Road', based on a widow who had turned her former home into a motel (does this sound familiar ?) and the contrasting struggle of her sister who had a much less prosperous background. ATV liked everything about the idea except the title but no one within the company could come up with anything better ! A local newspaper ran a competition for suggestions but even that failed to grip the

(Opposite) As Jill Richardson I kicked off the first programme by answering the telephone: 'Crossroads Motel, can I help you ?' The first person actually seen on screen, by the way, was Noele Gordon's mother, Jockey, who had come along to watch the historic recording and got roped in as Reg had forgotten to book an extra ! It could never happen these days – the Actors' Union, Equity, would see to that.

20 October 1964 – the first day of the very first 'Crossroads' rehearsal. Back row: me (Jill), Malcolm Young (Phillip Winter), Brian Kent (Dick Jarvis), Anthony Morton (Carlos). Seated: Roger Tonge (Sandy), Noele Gordon (Meg), Beryl Johnstone (Kitty Jarvis), David Fennell (Brian Jarvis).

public imagination and the prize had to be given away to charity! In the end Reg Watson himself dreamed up some ideas and 'Crossroads', though not a runaway hit, was the one people least objected to. From that unpromising beginning things could only get better and Reg embarked on the gargantuan task of finding actors to bring the roles of Meg and her children, and Kitty and Dick Jarvis to life.

Reg was a sweet man with an impish sense of humour, very strong on ideas and a great one for getting things done, but he was absolutely paranoid about secrecy. One of his recurring nightmares throughout the years he produced 'Crossroads' was the scripts being leaked, the cast talking to the press, or another soap stealing his ideas. In the beginning the secrecy that cloaked Crossroads was so great it nearly stopped me playing Jill at all.

When I got the call to audition I was working in repertory in York, playing Gilda in 'Alfie'. We had only started on the Monday and I had to ask the producer if I could leave the theatre early on Wednesday

(Above) Sandy and his friend Colin Warboys (Paul Hodgkinson) had the sort of on-off teenage friendship we've seen more recently with Beverley Grice and Sara – but Sandy always had to make the peace – he wanted Colin to put in a good word for him with his sister, Kate.

(Above right) 'Crossroads' showed from early days it was prepared to tackle difficult subjects when waitress Christine Fuller (Alex Marshall) joined the staff. Christine had an illegitimate baby – father unknown.

night to get to Birmingham for the audition. I already had a love/hate relationship with him over my fee. I'd been engaged at £13 a week but whenever I opened my little brown envelope it was always a pound short.

'Terrible takings, lovey,' he'd say, shaking his head and lighting up another of his evil-smelling Cuban cigarillos. 'You saw the house this afternoon, a couple of old age pensioners and a poodle. Tell you what, I'll make it up next week.' Of course, 'next week' never came.

When he flatly refused to let me go early, I was livid, especially as Gilda only appears in the first half, so that evening, still in my stage makeup, I slunk out of the theatre at the interval and when the rest of the cast were taking their curtain calls, I was speeding towards Birmingham in a second-class compartment !

Reg was pleased with my audition and offered me the part. All I knew about Jill was that she had completed a secretarial course in London and found a job on *Silhouette* magazine. (I could have done with taking some of their advice on slimming – I'm glad to say I've shed over two stone since 'Crossroads' started.) Jill was moving back to the Midlands to help her mother with the motel – and to avoid an affair with a married man. An omen for the disastrous course Jill's love life has taken ever since. . . .

I wasn't that worried when I didn't receive any written confirmation from Reg, but I was certainly rattled when I turned up at the studios the following week. Thanks to Reg's obsession with secrecy, the glamour-puss receptionist – all beehive and false eyelashes (it was 1964, remember) insisted there was no such programme as 'Crossroads'. I'd probably still be there arguing with her today if Reg hadn't burst through a set of double doors like a demented pixie and dragged me into the studio. He'd been looking for me for over an hour.

Reg had even more trouble finding someone to play the part of my young brother, Sandy. He'd auditioned hundreds of boy actors when, unannounced, a lad called Roger Tonge turned up at the Birmingham studios and caught Margaret French the Production Manager just as

All was to work out happily for Christine – Kings Oak milkman Ralph Palmer (Norman Jones) found enough bottle to ask her out, they started courting and were married in style – hiring a Rolls Royce for the wedding party to travel in, a far cry from Ralph's milk float.

Romance too for Brian Jarvis, son of Dick and Kitty. In April he got entangled with lovely widow Ruth Bailey (Pamela Greenhall) but she gently rebuffed him. Quickly recovering, he fell for his father's secretary, Janice Gifford (Carolyn Lister) and married her in November. The marriage survived her adultery with another man but not his alcoholism; he emerged from a drying out clinic to find himself divorced.

she was putting on her coat at the end of another weary day. To her undying credit, she patiently unlocked the filing cabinets, gave him a script, and told him to come back for an audition.

Roger duly turned up in his lunch hour – he was a Post Office clerk at the time, earning a princely £8 a week, and sweeping up backstage for the Post Office Dramatic Society, who wouldn't give him a part ! But his boyish looks and the froggy croak in his voice which seemed on the point of breaking for the entire seventeen years he was with the cast won him the role of Sandy and the hearts of millions. Roger's acting style has been called many things, at best 'individual' – but he and I represented the new naturalistic school of acting – in a way not acting at all, but being as lifelike and natural as possible. This didn't always go down well with older members of the cast who believed in a more rigorous approach but it helped establish a more relaxed style of acting on television and made 'Crossroads' one of the programmes people felt literally most at home with.

There was one role at least that Reg did not have to worry about filling – that of Meg Richardson, the lynch pin of the whole operation. He had been Noele Gordon's producer on 'Lunch Box' for eight years so he knew she could think on her feet and would never dry before the camera – something we've all become very adept at on 'Crossroads' over the years, we just keep talking when the sets fall down. . . Noele, though trained as an actress, had been a presenter for eight years and wondered how she'd cope with projecting a character again. What tempted her to take the part was Meg's name – her previous great success had been as Meg Brockie in 'Brigadoon', and you know how superstitious actors and actresses are !

Gradually all the other parts were filled. Initially there were only eight of us in the cast, the idea being that we would each work for six weeks and have a week off. But with only eight performers it was obvious that someone would have to work for seven weeks before their week off, someone for eight, someone for nine. . . . I completed eighty episodes without a break and by the time my holiday came I couldn't read the back of a cornflake packet without automatically trying to memorise it like a script. My break came at just the right time to save my sanity !

We had two weeks rehearsal then we were 'on the air'. We all hoped for an extension of our six weeks' contract but with the cautious optimism you learn as an actor, none of us counted on 'Crossroads' lasting more than two years, and thought we'd be doing well if it lasted that long. It just shows how wrong you can be – by Christmas, we'd been on the air for two months and made television history by being the world's first daily half-hour serial. We basked in the glory of a fairly prestigious 6 p.m. evening slot instead of being lost in the gathering gloom of the afternoon schedules. Millions of people were already embroiled in our goings-on and at Crossroads Motel business was booming.

Chef's Special

One of the most effective characters in the early days was Carlos the chef, an inspired performance from Anthony Morton. In fact all our chefs have been characters, not always in the best sense of the word. . . . When Tony Morton left (in the story Carlos was recalled to do his National Service, and back in Spain got the call to a monastic life, much to the surprise of his wife Josefina) the role of chef was taken over by William Avenell, who played the very strait-laced Mr Lovejoy. He called everyone by their surname except Josefina, and only when his rather raffish past came out and it transpired he had a daughter did he unbend enough to reveal his own Christian name – it was Gerald, by the way ! He made a great double act with David Lawton, who played Mr Booth, a character who ran an employment agency and, unable to find us a temporary chef, took on the job himself. As a character he also had his peculiarities, his catch phrase being 'If anyone wants me, I'll be in the storeroom.' He once spent ten months in there before he was seen again.

(Above) Chef and his 'little helper' Paul (Glyn Pritchard).

(Left) An omelette for Amy Turtle (Ann George).

Next came 'wee' Shughie McFee (Angus Lennie) whose Burns Night Suppers became something of a legend. Today the tradition is upheld in 'Chef', or 'Big Chef' as he is known, the brilliant creation of scriptwriter Andy Rashleigh. And Chef is in fact played by . . . Andy Rashleigh. A dipsomaniac naturist who terrorises young Paul, 'Chef' has varied musical tastes, being a fan of both 'Oklahoma' and The Yetties.

(Above) Meg and Shughie McFee (Angus Lennie).

2
Early Days

From the outset, the schedule for 'Crossroads' has made working on a North Sea oil rig seem like relaxation.

In the early days we were shown Monday to Friday so the cast had the equivalent of a different full-length play to memorise every single week. The programme had a longer slot time (a full twenty-five minutes), there were fewer characters and longer speeches, which were much harder to learn. And that was on top of a schedule where rehearsal and recording took up six days out of seven !

Our first rehearsal room was in Rutland House over ATV's offices in

Home is the sailor, home from the sea – Meg's brother, Andy Fraser (Ian Patterson) (below) came to Kings Oak to be best man at the wedding of his naval friend Tom Yorke (Gavin Hamilton) to Joyce Hepworth (Jan Butlin) (right). Within the year, he too had found true love in the village.

the centre of Birmingham – we used to sit on the stairs and learn our lines which must have been very distracting for the staff ! Downstairs, men in grey suits pored over profit-and-loss accounts while on the first floor, in a huge room with half a dozen chairs and a lot of ashtrays, we acted out kidnap attempts, death threats and the usual everyday stuff of motel life. After six months we moved to rather cosier rooms in Bradford Street, this time sandwiched between an import/export business and a model agency, close by Birmingham's Fish Market. Three years ago we moved up the road to our present quarters which have all the Victorian attic qualities of Rutland House, and a leaky roof into the bargain – so you can see what a glamorous life we lead.

At Bradford Street, we soon established a routine. Noele, who was a sort of dowager Queen Mum figure to us all, naturally had place of honour, a chair opposite the door, and woe betide anyone who unwittingly sat there ! Nolly would say nothing, in fact she would be

Meg's good friend Ruth Bailey, tragically widowed when her husband Gerald was killed in a hit-and-run accident, decided to take the plunge into marriage again with Meg's seafaring brother. Retired from the sea, but still attracted to foreign parts, they set up a travel agency together. This union marked 'Crossroads' 500th episode.

In September, Meg met the man of her dreams, Hugh Mortimer (John Bentley). She could not then know it would be ten long years before they would marry.

(Opposite) Romance was in the air for Jill with Phillip Winter. When she got hopelessly drunk on their first date, he turned out to be a true gentleman.

perfectly charming, but her compressed lips said it all, and whenever possible we had to warn people off – rather like Darby's chair in the Staff Room ! I used to sit at the rickety centre table and spread my things about me, but after ten years of suffering scripts liberally sprinkled with coffee, I graduated to an armchair, and when Noele left, as senior member of the company I dared to claim her chair and took over the Hot Seat !

Opposite Noele's chair was the wall-mounted telephone and next to it – fatal – a mirror. Actors are always neurotically on the phone to their agents, chasing money or bookings and the temptation to preen in the mirror, tidy your hair or examine the crow's feet was too great. Neville Hughes, who played Peter Hope, the vicar, was a superb mimic (as Paul Henry is today) and would have everyone else in the room in stitches with his take-offs of whoever was on the phone – the only person oblivious was the victim. And we needed to let off steam, because we were working like crazy.

Our working week started on a Friday, when we would block through five episodes, that is, walk them through in the rehearsal room with doorways and pieces of furniture marked out in tape on the floor. On Saturday, starting at ten, we'd go through the whole lot again, working all day with no break for lunch. I always aimed to know my lines by Saturday – Sunday was our precious day off and I didn't want 'Crossroads' scripts nagging at me ! By Monday we were ready for a Tech. (Technical) Run before lunch and the Producer's Run in the afternoon – definitely no scripts by this stage ! On Tuesdays – bliss – we had the morning off – then it was into the studio for a walk through on set, then a stagger-through with cameras. This was when the director found out that his brilliant shot wouldn't work because a microphone or a dead body was in the way (there were a lot of corpses at 'Crossroads' in those days), so you had a complete new lot of moves to remember – all part of life's rich tapestry for an actor. This was followed by a proper run-through, then a dress run, then a take of the entire episode, straight off, in scene order. And this was how we worked until three years ago, a terrible ordeal for anyone new to the cast used to the luxuries of rehearse-record.

These early episodes were recorded on 'telecine' but we were always so impoverished we couldn't afford editing time. If you made a hideous fluff in Scene One there was time to go back and do it again, but towards the end of the episode, as the forty-five minutes allocated for the recording ticked away, you just had to press on regardless. I'll never forget a scene I did with Noele in the sitting room. She had to put some papers in the safe, then come back on and pour some tea. On rehearsal, the safe behaved beautifully, of course, but on the take, as soon as she closed the door, it swung open again. Slamming it shut and leaning casually against it, Noele launched into her tea-pouring speech from the far wall . . . and the next speech, and the next. Finally I realised what had happened and poured the tea myself !

You'd think with that work schedule all we'd have been fit for in the evenings was a cup of cocoa and an early night, but far from it. It was the swinging sixties – even in Birmingham – and we had a ball. We were out at clubs and parties and pop concerts practically every night. A lot of the cast clicked instantly with that personal chemistry you just can't cultivate – though I think our way of working helped. As we went for continuous action – as if it were a live programme –

Real wedding bells for a change! Most of the cast of 'Crossroads' turned up to my wedding in May 1965. Anthony Morton was best man and Alex Marshall a bridesmaid. Left to right: Anthony Howard (Victor Amos), Malcolm Young (Phillip),

'Crossroads' had the real company feel of a stage show. And the regulars always took it upon themselves to make newcomers feel at home – showing them the ropes in the studio, taking them out for vast Chinese meals. There were plenty of actors who came in rather condescendingly for a part lasting a couple of weeks and went away amazed at our stamina – on the set and off.

Noele Gordon (Meg), John Bentley (Hugh), Tim Jones (Director), me, Anthony Morton (Carlos), Alex Marshall (Christine) and my family.

Ken Dodd and David Jason both appeared in early episodes . . . though David Jason denies it !

3

Work Hard, Play Hard

*I*f we worked hard, we played hard too and we had such a lot of laughs on and off the set it helped us cope with the stresses and strains of such a punishing schedule.

One of my first big stories as the young, impressionable Jill was my fling with Philip Winter, the motel handyman. In one scene, I was waiting for him outside the motel with Portia, the Great Dane who belonged to actor David Fennell, who played Brian Jarvis. Portia was a regular fixture on 'Crossroads' for some years – so much so that when an English teacher set the question 'Who was Portia?' in a paper, half the class supposedly wrote 'The dog in Crossroads!' I was holding Portia on a leash when she decided to go walkies and headed towards Reception. But to avoid reflections, there wasn't any glass in the doors and Portia glided through – if Great Danes can glide – in a ghostly fashion, leaving me the option of wrestling with the door frame with her inside, or ducking down and materialising through glass myself.

We had some real practical jokers in the cast and the dress run was a superb time for a bit of fun. Anthony Howard gave a great performance as the baddy Victor Amos who cheated Dick Jarvis, and it was decided Victor would get his just deserts by having a heart attack. The final dramatic shot to signify he was no more was to be his hand falling limply to the floor. Tony duly 'died', the camera homed in on his hand, only to find it clutching a card reading 'Available for pantomime!'

Another time, Alan Coleman and Tim Jones, the two original directors, decided to play a trick on Reg. We were doing a murder story but in those days the IBA was very strict and on no account could a dead body be seen on screen when there might be children watching. To get round this, we decided that the dead man should be identified by his signet ring, one with a sinister skull on it, so whenever he was seen buying a drink or whatever, the camera zoomed in on the ring. On the day of the 'murder', Tim and Alan hired Tina, one of the Twycross Zoo chimps from the PG Tips commercials, so that when the dead man's hand was seen, which was all we were allowed to show, it was a hairy chimp's hand sporting the ring. For a moment

David Fennell with his dog Portia, no respecter of sets!

Reg seriously contemplated seeing his doctor to see if he was suffering from overwork – before light dawned and he realised the Crossroads crew was at it again !

But it wasn't all fun and frolic – we were, after all, making a drama serial that people were watching in their millions and really beginning to identify with. Romance is the true stuff of soap and when Brian Jarvis and Janice Gifford married, the service was conducted by my brother at his church in Smethwick. Afterwards there was much discussion as to whether the actors, David Fennell and Carolyn Lister, might really be married to each other as he was an ordained Minister ! Another love story which caught the public's imagination was the proposal of the handsome young vicar, Peter Hope, to Motel waitress Marilyn Gates. (Peter had taken over from the Reverend Guy Atkins, played by Arnold Ridley of 'Dad's Army' fame.) Marilyn thought she wasn't 'good enough' for him and while he was still trying to persuade her she would be excellent at bridge teas and opening bazaars, the London region dropped 'Crossroads' from its schedules. There was an absolute furore and for six months the poor deprived viewers in the South East didn't know whether Marilyn and Peter made it to the altar or not. The Prime Minister's wife, Mrs Mary Wilson, got involved in the campaign to restore it to the screen, and Thames management

(Below left) Brian Jarvis and Janice Gifford hoping their marriage is made in heaven.

(Below right) 'Crossroads' again broached a touchy subject when vicar Peter Hope (Neville Hughes) proposed to waitress Marilyn Gates (Sue Nicholls), former pop singer and ex-beauty queen. She did not think she was good enough for him but thanks to a little subtle subterfuge by his mother, Tish, herself a former showgirl, stage name Venetia Dawn, true love prevailed and in 1968 they were married.

Marilyn Gates charmed by the native pipes.

finally caved in under pressure, but for six months London trailed behind the rest of the country in the storyline !

Sue Nicholls, who played Marilyn and is now Gail Tilsley's Mum in 'Coronation Street', was great fun to work with and I really felt for her very soon after 'Crossroads' started. It was the election night of Harold Wilson's great Labour victory and we were watching the results come through at a studio party.

'And now we're going over to Peterborough for the result,' said the presenter. 'No, I'm sorry [listening to his earpiece], my mistake, there's going to be a recount.'

Poor Sue was in agony. Her father, Sir Harmar Nicholls, was Conservative MP for Peterborough, and she had to sit through three recounts that night until he scraped home by about six votes !

I was really sorry when Sue left the cast – it was one of those strange cases of life imitating art. As Marilyn, Sue was intent on a career as a nightclub singer and Reg asked Tony Hatch, who composed

Meg and Marilyn ponder the wisdom of a camel ride.

the original 'Crossroads' theme, to write her a ballad to sing in the programme. This was 'Where Will You Be ?' which was released as a commercial disc and got to Number 17. Sue herself then decided she wanted a career in the pop world and no-one could persuade her to stay. Reg recast the part but the vicar and his wife merged more and more into the background till they were banished to do missionary work in Africa.

There was a time when 'Crossroads' itself came 'Out of Africa'. One of the highlights of the sixties for many of the cast was the time they spent filming in Tunisia, where Meg had gone to advise on the opening of a new hotel after 'Crossroads' had been largely destroyed by a wartime bomb which exploded when workmen dug it up. Unfortunately, someone had to stay back and mind the shop, so Jill was left behind – not for the first time. I missed out on Torremolinos, I missed out on Tunisia and I missed out on Paris. It wasn't until 1983 that I made my first trip abroad with the programme – to Venice for my honeymoon with Adam and reunion with Meg – but it was

Carlos tries to trade Marilyn for a camel.

magical, and I was glad I'd saved myself for it !

By the end of the decade, 'Crossroads' was well established as one of the most popular programmes on British television and it stayed that way by following very strict guidelines. The writers' 'Bible' from 1969 makes thought-provoking reading. . . . The very first entry, under 'General Writing Points', is categorical: 'There is no cigarette smoking, even by villains'. Sex had to be very delicately handled – terms like 'sleeping around' and 'shacking up', the guide states, are 'tabu'. And 'Crossroads' was also very sensitive to the make-up of its audience. The 'Bible' reveals that calling someone a 'basket' let alone a 'bastard' would upset 8% of viewers, to 'welsh' would displease the 5.5% of viewers from the principality while 4.6% (the Irish contingent) would be offended by someone getting in 'a paddy'. Even to say someone had been 'gipped' would hurt .01% of viewers, presumably watching 'Crossroads' in their gaily-painted Romany caravans.

What 'Crossroads' did provide in a large quantity was harmless escapism for millions of viewers, mostly women who wanted to forget about their own domestic troubles. By comparison to the derring-do at the Motel, their worries over the washing machine packing up or little Johnny's measles must have seemed trivial indeed. And for the next twenty years the 'Crossroads' formula did not change much. The people you met at 'Crossroads' were black or white (not a phrase that would have gone down well in 1969 !). The 'good' ones – Benny or Jill, for example, were warm and likeable. Dreadful things happened to them but (luckily for me) they survived. 'Bad' characters, on the other hand, got their come-uppance. Situations were much worse than real life, but the characters were much less complicated – reassuring viewing at the end of a busy day.

The cast gather round for 'Crossroads' fifth anniversary in 1969. Left to right: Carolyn Lister (seated), William Avenell, Susan Hanson, Peter Brookes, me, Noele Gordon, Brian Kent (rear), Roger Tonge, Joy Andrews, Diane Keen (seated), Michael Osborne (rear), David Fennell.

4

A Way of Life

As sixties psychedelia faded away and the Flower Children settled down, so did 'Crossroads' and the regular cast built quite a civilised existence round the horrendous working schedule. The civilising influence was largely due to the arrival of Ronald Allen to play suave Motel director David Hunter. A real heart-throb, Ronnie is also a true gentleman and it was refreshing to meet someone who stood up when a lady entered the room, opened doors and so on – luckily there were no ardent feminists in the cast! At the time I lived in Kew and a group of us would commute on the train, learning our lines on the way up, relaxing with a sort of grown-up picnic on the way back. We took turns bringing the wine and sandwiches, and the buffet car staff got to know us and were always ready with the ice! Two of our directors, Jack Barton and Rollo Gamble, also travelled by train and used to keep us entertained with a fund of stories.

In 1972 Reg decided to return to Australia and the search was on for a new producer. As usual, the cast were among the last to hear but we were delighted when the job went to Jack Barton. He was a sort of benign Father Christmas figure to us all. When I was splitting up from my first husband, Tim, in 1970, I met Jack in the studio lift and, seeing how upset I was, he let me pour out my woes and helped arrange a fantastically heavy workload for me for the next six months. If I hadn't had the discipline of working I could have gone under and it was thanks to Jack I came through the pain and out the other side.

One of Reg's last decisions before he left for 'down under' was to get Jill married again. He was very disappointed Jill's first marriage had failed and he wanted my second choice of husband to be a success and fit in with the rest of the cast. He told me the sort of chap he had in mind for Jill – a no-nonsense, working man – and I immediately suggested Edward Clayton, who'd been at drama school with me, and who lived, conveniently, in Stoke-on-Trent. Another reason for marrying Jill off was that at the heart of every soap there's supposed to be a strong family unit. The Jarvis family had gradually been whittled down to just Brian and Janice, and a lot of the action had moved to the Motel. Reg thought it was about time the Richardsons

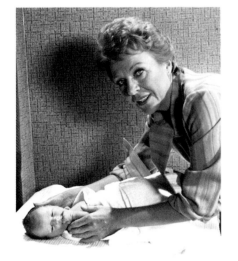

High drama at the motel in 1972 when Meg delivered Sheila Harvey's baby boy on the dining room floor. More recently, Charlie Mycroft (Graham Seed) and Tara (Tara Shaw) were in at the birth of a guest's baby – Mum Katie named it after Tara and invited her to be godmother.

came down to earth so Jill's boutique went bust and she fell in love with the electrician who came to mend the wiring – Stan Harvey.

The biggest joke about the Harvey household was the set, which for some reason had been constructed without a proper entrance. It consisted of a living room with kitchen area and the only doorway supposedly led upstairs. Directly in front of this door was a sofa which you literally had to climb over to get in or out of the room. If more than one person had to go upstairs, you were both perched on top of a tiny flight of steps clinging on to the wall until the scene ended, trying not to giggle.

Scenes in the Harvey house were inevitably one long meal – the entire first half of one episode was given over to me cooking, serving up and us eating. The only snag was that the cooker wasn't wired up, so the prop boys had to poke bits of cooked bacon on to the grill pan through a hole in the set while I was out of shot, or whip the frying pan off me and replace it with another so I could trill merrily 'Grub's up !' By the time we got to eat these never-ending meals, everything was stone cold. It's no wonder Stan took to spending so much time in Germany given the standard of the food he was served at home !

As Stan and Jill we eventually got our own flat and gave a dinner party for Brian and Janice Jarvis. It was a very long and complicated scene and we all had to concentrate very hard, giving each other kicks

Breakfast with the Harveys – no wonder I look so miserable, I spent half my life in the kitchen !

under the table and surreptitious nods when it was the next person's turn to speak. When the scene was finally over, David Fennell (Brian) was so relieved he sprang up, turned round . . . and walked smack into the set. With an enormous crash the pictures fell off the wall. We all collapsed but thankfully the camera had moved off us and we were just a distant crash in the next scene.

The happiest time for Stan and Jill was the birth of Sarah Jane, played by my own daughter, Sorrel. The story came about because I was pregnant in real life but the idea was to wait and see if I had a boy or a girl before writing the detail into the script. By coincidence, the very day Stan was to announce 'Jill's had the baby' (cue the closing music) I went into labour. Ted's scene was to be recorded at 6.30 pm and Sorrel was conveniently born an hour earlier so the second phone call my husband David made – after one to the grandparents – was to the studio. There was a swift script change and Sarah Jane had arrived !

(Above) It wasn't hard to look happy for this photo – baby Sarah Jane is my own real-life daughter, Sorrel.

They say you should never work with children or animals – from my experience I would add 'especially your own'. I don't know how Lucille Ball did it. In fact, Sorrel was never a problem on set apart from a loathing of the tannoy in the dressing rooms. I had to park her pram so well out of earshot I often missed my call as well. On screen,

(Below) One of my favourite photographs of myself, Sorrell, Noele and Roger.

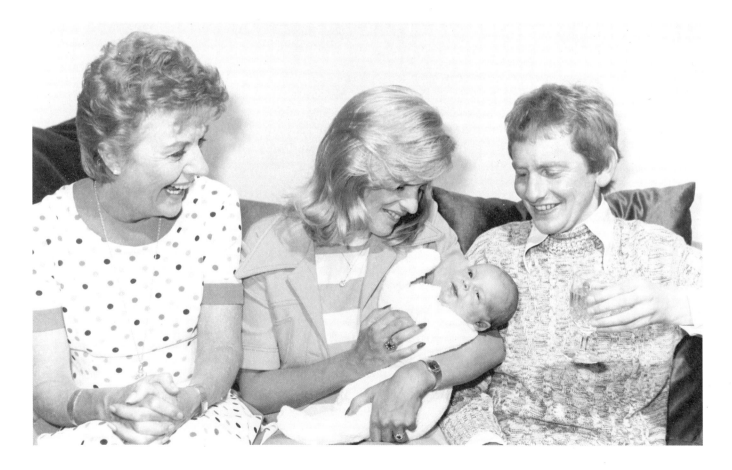

she was super except when she was sick all over me on a take, and one Christmas scene we did when she sat in a high chair and ate everything in sight, including the crackers. Another Christmas, when she was two or three, we were opening presents round the tree and I was having a conversation with Meg and Amy Turtle while watching Sarah Jane out of the corner of my eye. For a moment my attention was distracted and in that split second Sorrel toddled over to the coffee table and downed a glass of brandy. Luckily it was only studio brandy, gravy browning, but I got hundreds of letters telling me what a dreadful mother I was.

Another of Reg's final decisions was to paralyse Sandy. This all stemmed from a real-life car crash Roger Tonge had been involved in. Roger broke his arm and needed eighty stitches in his face and he was lying in his hospital bed drugged up to the eyeballs and feeling very sorry for himself when Reg arrived. Cheery as ever, Reg plonked down a bunch of grapes and a pile of papers. 'Rewrites,' he said brightly. 'Learn them by Monday, OK?' He'd written round Sandy's awful appearance by explaining he'd bumped into a plate-glass door! Roger, bless him, couldn't help laughing. 'At least I thought I'd get the week off!' he said.

In truth, Reg was so shaken by the sight of Roger arriving at the studios in a wheelchair that he filed it away for future reference but Sandy's paralysis was actually a brilliant idea that went wrong. Reg had wanted him to walk again after six months but somehow in the scripts he was given such dire injuries there was no such possibility and all of us – above all Roger – had to live with it. Sandy's accident certainly made us realise just how difficult it is for disabled people to lead a normal life. Doors on the set had to be widened as the wheelchair couldn't get through. Ramps had to be built where there were steps When Sandy came into a set we physically had to move the furniture to accommodate him. When in later years they decided Sandy could walk with calipers, Roger had all the problems that ensue. The calipers rubbed his legs and made them bleed and it was a lesson to all of us seeing the courage it takes for the disabled to face life in a wheelchair or out. And the story enabled us to touch on all sorts of sensitive issues – would Sandy as an otherwise healthy young man be able to enjoy what doctors would call a 'full sex life'?

One concrete result of Sandy's paralysis was the 'Crossroads Care Attendant Scheme' which was started in Rugby in 1974. The idea behind it is so sensible and so simple you wonder why no one else thought of it. The 'Crossroads' scheme enables 'carers' to take a break leaving the disabled person in the capable hands of a fully trained attendant. It was such a brilliant idea that it was taken up nationwide and is now an official EEC charity.

When Jack took over, the Sandy story was a gift to him because as well as the usual stuff of soap – births, deaths, marriages and so on – Jack thought the medium should have a message, and believed

Amy Turtle was the eyes and ears of the motel – and the village. Here Mr Booth alerts Tish Hope (Joy Andrews) that they are not alone. The other eavesdropper is postman and part-time barman Vince Parker (Peter Brookes).

'Crossroads' was the ideal vehicle for getting across information in a dramatic and entertaining way. Under Jack's auspices we tackled all sorts of sensitive issues in, I hope, a way that wasn't heavy-handed. We covered racial prejudice with Joe and Trina MacDonald, agoraphobia and kidney disease with Jim and Muriel Baines, gambling with David Hunter, heroin addiction with the Maguires' son, Pete, as well as tranquilliser addiction. That was my story and a pretty miserable one it was too. I had to crunch handfuls of those tiny mints (which upset my stomach) in place of pills, and spent a lot of time swaddled in blankets because one of the withdrawal symptoms is cold and uncontrollable shivering. Under the studio lights, however, I used to get incredibly hot and while my teeth were chattering I was dripping with perspiration! More cheerfully, Nina, a Down's Syndrome child came into the programme so we could show our viewers there's nothing shocking about such a handicap and on a happier note still, *in vitro* fertilisation was a success for Glenda and Kevin Banks with the arrival of their test-tube baby, Katy-Louise.

In this way, Jack built on the sure foundations he had inherited from Reg. The 'Crossroads' formula, though hard to define, was very successful and Jack was determined not to upset the balance. He often experimented with a new character by trying him or her out for a while and, depending on how the actor got on with the rest of the cast and coped with the schedule, would then be brought back in a bigger role. Many joined in this way, like Sally Adcock who played Jane Smith, a very popular character at the end of the seventies, and of course Tony Adams, who was tried out in a small part and came back as Adam Chance. Stan Stennett, the comedian who became a regular as Sid Hooper was first seen as a gunman on the run! Vera Downend (Zeph Gladstone) who ran the hairdressing salon, and gardener Sam Carne (Jack Woolgar) were two more of the warm, lovable characters from those days. The cast was full of people who came for a week and stayed for years – but we liked it that way.

(Opposite) Sandy recovering from his car accident, which left him a paraplegic.

Famous Faces

Jack Barton introduced many new characters. They joined the thousands of actors who have checked into the Motel over the years . . . Malcolm McDowell, for instance, who made his name in the film *A Clockwork Orange* played Crispin Ryder, a PR consultant in 'Crossroads'. Others include Nicholas Ball ('Hazell'), Don Henderson ('Bulman'), Sneh Gupta ('The Far Pavilions') and Jeffrey Holland ('Hi-de-Hi'). Elaine Paige, who created the part of 'Evita' on stage, appeared way back in Episode 880 of 'Crossroads' as Caroline Winthrop !

(Above) Clifford Layton (Johnny Briggs) up to no good . . . with Diane (Susan Hanson), Vera (Zeph Gladstone), and the inevitable P.C.

(Opposite above) Walter Soper (Max Wall) and Sid Hooper (Stan Stennett) share a surreptitious smoke.

(Opposite below) At Meg and Hugh's wedding Noel's great friend, Larry Grayson, was a surprise chauffeur.

Many actors who have appeared in 'Crossroads' have defected to our rival 'Coronation Street' – Sue Nicholls, Johnny Briggs, Fred Feast, Bryan Moseley, Reginald Marsh and Gina Maher.

A host of comedians have also made guest appearances in 'Crossroads'. Nolly's great friend Larry Grayson booked in as a guest and complained about ferrets in the woodwork while Max Wall, in a 'straight' part as Walter Soper, Arthur Brownlow's cousin, soon teamed up with another comedian, Stan Stennett (Sid Hooper). Funny man Don MacLean featured early on as a member of Benny Wilmot's pop group – the brilliantly named Georgie Saint and the Dragons!

5
The End of the Beginning

*J*ack's commitment to 'Crossroads' soon paid off and in the early seventies the programme could do no wrong – we were one of the most consistently popular programmes on television. Nolly won the *TV Times* award for the Favourite Female Personality and Most Compulsive Character no less than eight times until in the end they asked her not to stand to give someone else a chance ! She was then elevated to the *TV Times* Hall of Fame – the first award winner to receive this honour. The programme itself won *The Sun* award for the Best TV Series for three years running – 1973, 1974 and 1975. To the cast this was something of a miracle because 'Crossroads' wasn't fully networked until 1972 when Granada finally caved in and took it, and even then we were transmitted across the country at different times. ATV showed us at 6.00 pm, Tyne Tees at two minutes past, Granada at five past, while most of the rest of the world had to wait till 6.35 ! (Apart from Channel and the South West where you could tune in as early as 5.20 !) We were constantly receiving letters from shop and factory workers who could not get home in time and this inconsistency put us at a real disadvantage compared with other soaps. Even up to two years ago the episode that was seen in, say, Leicester on a Thursday wasn't seen in London until the following Monday, so there was no end-of-the-week feeling. This made it easy for the critics to say there was no sense of time or place in 'Crossroads' – how could there be ?

We still had a pathetically small budget – we used to provide all our own clothes – and to save replacing sets, characters were always moving in and out of each other's houses. In one scene David Hunter, who was taking over Meg's cottage, had gone round to inspect it with his current ladyfriend and had to peer up the chimney, whereupon a bit of soot would fall down. After the dress run, the director's note to the prop boys was 'Not enough soot ! I could hardly see it !' On the take, eager to oblige, they emptied a whole bag of soot down the chimney and the immaculate David was absolutely covered. When Ronnie Allen finally came up spluttering he looked like Bojangles – all you could see were the whites of his eyes. We had some fun at that

Glamorous Barbara Brady (Sue Lloyd) seemed an odd choice as housekeeper to Lloyd Munro. But novelist Barbara only took the job to research a book.

cottage. In one scene Meg and I had gone round for drinks, and our hostess Barbara (Sue Lloyd) was wearing a glamorous silky dress. There was a leather sofa in the sitting room and she perched on the arm until we realised she was gradually slipping further and further out of shot. Finally she slid gracefully on to the floor and did the rest of the scene from there !

Ronnie had another funny moment when, in a dramatic storyline, his ex-wife Rosemary, played by Janet Hargreaves, jealous of his engagement to Barbara, came and took a pot-shot at him. As I've said, we all provided our own clothes but on this rare occasion, as the jacket would end up covered in gore, stage manager Liz Stern, who has also been with us since Day One, persuaded Wardrobe to kit Ronnie out. On the take, as soon as he saw Janet's finger on the trigger, Ronnie burst the little pouch of studio blood under his arm – but the gun didn't go off ! Wardrobe had to find yet another jacket to fit but that wasn't what held up the scene – it was the cast, helpless with laughter. . . .

Backstage it was always a scramble to get dressed and made up in time, and we had to dart into Make-up between scenes and hope for the best. Sue Hanson was once called rather earlier than she expected to do one scene and as I watched on the monitor I thought there was something rather odd about her hair. She'd only got a couple of rollers in ! But because of time constraints the scene went out and I suppose everyone at home thought that, being Diane, she'd left for work in such a hurry she'd forgotten to take them out !

A more familiar scene of the late seventies was David, Barbara, Meg, myself and sometimes Adam in the office, talking business. We all used to dread these scenes because none of us really understood the ins and outs of the business world (nor, I suspect, did the writers). We used to get through the scene by nodding at each other when it was the next person's turn to speak and Ronnie was especially naughty at trying to corpse you when you were delivering some solemn line about 'creative accounting' – and I usually succumbed !

As a contrast to the motel, and as a breath of fresh air, came the farm and the introduction of a character who, for many, has come to symbolise 'Crossroads' – Benny, played by Paul Henry. Viewers took Benny to their hearts and one of the most successful stories (Jack's social conscience showing again) was Diane teaching him to read. Through the farm, too, we met Doris Luke, played by Kathy Staff, best known as Nora Batty in the BBC's 'Last of the Summer Wine'. And there were other new characters, too. The recent criticism of the Grices when they arrived in the village amused me because when the Brownlows were introduced it was a very similar scenario – we used to call them 'The Glums' ! Kath Brownlow (Pamela Vezey) became a warm and much-loved character but the family set-up was originally very down-beat, even depressing. The point was to give a contrast to life at the motel but Nolly, for one, loathed the Brownlows when they were introduced and she was not alone !

But these were happy years – comfy, secure, settled. We were recording four programmes a week and showing three, so we had enough in hand for us to enjoy thirteen weeks' holiday a year – a long break at Christmas, Easter and in the summer. It was almost like being back at school. Life was full and busy but organised. Ronnie often used to say to me, 'We're so lucky, you know, Jane. This can't go on.' How right he was.

(Above) When Benny (Paul Henry) came to work on the farm, Diane ('Miss Diane' to Benny), took him under her wing and taught him to read, an act he repaid with undying devotion.

(Opposite above) Benny quickly got to grips with work on the farm. His gruff but kind hearted 'gaffer', Ed Lawton, was played by Thomas Heathcote.

(Opposite below) The dreaded Brownlows – Ron (Ian Liston), Glenda (Lynette McMorrough), Arthur (Peter Hill) and Kath (Pamela Vezey).

Wedding Bells

(Above) Jill's wedding to village electrician Stan Harvey (Edward Clayton).

(Above right) On the brink of a new life, Meg was radiant but enjoyed just three brief years of happiness. Hugh died of a heart attack after being kidnapped by terrorists.

(Right) Diane Lawton and village postie Vince Parker tied the knot in 1971.

(Opposite) The highlight of the seventies and the Wedding of the Century was Meg's long awaited marriage to Hugh Mortimer. There wasn't a dry eye in the house as Meg and Hugh finally made it up the aisle for the blessing at Birmingham Cathedral.

(Opposite) In 1981 Royal Wedding fever swept Kevin Banks (David Moran) and Glenda Brownlow to the altar.

(Left) David Hunter (Ronald Allen) married Barbara Brady in 1980 – the first 'Crossroads' wedding at Tanworth-in-Arden and another bitterly cold day on location.

(Below) Jill's wedding to Adam in 1983. It was a wonderful day – and sunny, for once ! We raised our glasses to the future . . . 'for better, for worse' ! From back left: David Hunter, Barbara Hunter, Sid Hooper, Diane Hunter, Joe MacDonald (Carl Andrews), Mavis Hooper (Charmian Eyre), Kath Brownlow, Sharon Metcalfe (Carolyn Jones), me and Adam (Tony Adams), the vicar, and not forgetting Sarah Jane.

6
The Beginning of the End

It was 1.00 on a Sunday morning when I was woken by the telephone. On the other end was a newspaperman who kept going on and on about my mother. Only half awake, I wasn't really taking it in until he said something about my mother dying. I started to panic until I realised he was talking about my screen mother, Meg. I told him he was talking nonsense and put the phone down but I didn't sleep very well for what remained of the night. When I turned up for work next day Noele told me she'd been sacked. She had known for two weeks and the first person she'd told was Tony Adams, to whom she was very close.

I couldn't believe it. Meg sacked from her own motel? To most people Noele Gordon *was* 'Crossroads' and without her I didn't think there was a future for any of us.

Everyone asks 'Why did it happen?' I don't know – I can only surmise. The franchise for the Midlands was being taken over by Central with its modern, up-to-date image. One of the programmes they inherited from ATV was 'Crossroads'. True, it was cheap to make – we still did hardly any location filming – and it generated lots of advertising revenue but Central never really wanted it and maybe they thought that by removing Meg, the lynch-pin at the centre of the structure, 'Crossroads' would collapse of its own accord.

I don't know how we got through the next few months. Nolly had six months of her contract left to run, though in the end she was released early because she had the chance to do 'Gypsy' at Leicester. The cast felt doubly insecure because at first we thought Jack would go with her. But he was determined to stay on and fight for what remained, so the great game began with the Press – how was Meg to go?

After many secret meetings and memos marked 'Strictly Confidential', it was decided to burn down the motel, the mystery being 'Was Meg inside?' For authenticity, we actually took the old set to an airfield for a rare and expensive night shoot so that recognisable bits of scenery could be seen going up in smoke. Naturally there were hundreds of fire tenders and water hoses standing by to comply with all the

*Meg slumbers unaware of the inferno
at the Motel . . .*

Reception – before . . .

. . . and after.

The film which was never shown –
Meg's mock funeral. I had to cry for
20 minutes until the Press helicopter
flew away.

safety regulations – but, miraculously, no Press. Then I was booked for another morning on location – me, a coffin and hundreds of flowers. There was no script, they just wanted to film me crying. I wept for twenty minutes in all because of a Press helicopter which, having got wind of what was going on, buzzed about over our heads making filming impossible because it interfered with the sound levels, but I had to keep crying until it went away – pretty gruelling – and in the end, of course, the film was never shown.

Then came another mysterious telephone call, this time from Jack. At the last minute and with two weeks' notice, they'd decided to change the end and I was summoned down to Southampton for a weekend shoot. Meg was to be spared, and was about to sail off on the QE2 to New York to settle near her little grandson, Matthew. When we got to the dock the ship had not yet arrived, so I had to turn on the tears again and they filmed me crying on the quay. When the ship eventually berthed we went on board with our cables, cameras and all the rest of the gear and installed ourselves in the very best suite. There I had to say my public farewells to Noele, a very difficult scene for both of us and one which left us very choked. But as usual with 'Crossroads' there was an element of farce. All our lights in such a small space made the cabin very hot and the automatic sprinklers came on. Cunard executives were going mad – the carpet had been specially woven at a cost of about £100 per square foot and they were terrified of it being ruined!

Finally the QE2 sailed off with its real passengers on board – and Noele too, of course, waving from the deck. It was a very splendid occasion with the brass band playing in full regalia, and Tony Adams sailed up in his little boat 'Seaway' for moral support. There was no way the ship could turn round so Noele actually had to sail to the first port of call, Cherbourg, and fly back from there. I believe a part of Jack really enjoyed all this subterfuge – at Southampton he even donned a false moustache and when stopped by a posse of journalists and questioned he gave our stage manager's name, Wolfenden! There was another irony back at the studios. Some time before, Noele had had her dressing room re-papered with a design of waves. Sue Lloyd, who is a brilliant artist, said to her jokingly that it cried out for a boat so she drew one in, with Tony Adams at the helm, Noele waving and even a little Rolls Royce sketched in on the back. Little did we know. . . .

When Noele opened in 'Gypsy' we turned out in force – we occupied the entire front two rows of the circle. It was a marvellous night. Noele came alive on that stage – she was triumphant. You can't define star quality but whatever it is, she had it and a light went out of 'Crossroads' when she left. Incredibly, to those of us who remained, the show chugged on.

(Top) A sad farewell for Meg and Jill on board the QE2.

(Above) A cheery wave as Meg – and Noele – departed for a new life.

7
Absent Friends

*N*oele and I had become great friends over the years but when I first realised I was going to have to play opposite her I can honestly say I was terrified. She was something of a legend even in those days.

Born on Christmas Day, no-one quite knows when, Noele was brought up in a strict Scottish Presbyterian household by her mother who was known as Jockey because of her small build. Her father, a ship's engineer, was often away from home and mother and daughter built up a close relationship which lasted throughout their lives. As a child Noele lived in East Ham, London and made her first stage appearance at the age of two and a half, singing 'Dear Little Jammy Face !'. Enrolled at RADA when she was only fifteen, Noele went into the theatre as understudy in the comedy 'Aren't Men Beasts' at the Strand Theatre, London. All four female leads fell ill in turn, so Noele had a shot at all the parts but her great triumph was the role of Meg Brockie in 'Brigadoon' – she gave almost 1,000 performances. Her first connection with TV came when Logie Baird used her for his pioneer experiments in colour, attracted by her black hair and blue eyes. In the early fifties Noele realised that television was the coming thing and took herself off to America to learn about production techniques. Back in England she was offered a trainee director's job with ATV women's programmes but was soon in front of the cameras. She was the dare-devil girl who would try anything, a sort of 1950s Anneka Rice, learning to skin-dive and to fly. Then came 'Tea with Noele Gordon', later 'Lunch Box', and finally 'Crossroads'.

'Crossroads' was a *real* crossroads for Noele's career. Not only was she returning to acting after presenting for eight years, but she had to face up to the fact that in the serial she had a grown-up daughter. Like many women Noele was sensitive about her age but once she got used to the idea of being a mother she rather liked it. She had grown up in an age when women had to choose between marriage and a career and it's true to say that Roger and I were the son and daughter she never had. We took to calling her 'Mother' – and to the rest of the cast she was (without the sinister connotations) 'The Godmother'.

Mother and daughter, the best of friends – Noele and Jockey.

(Left) Meg and Sandy – mother and son in the mid-Seventies.

(Below left) Nolly loved her public – here she signs an autograph for a young fan.

(Below) 1980 . . . our last Christmas together, though we didn't know it.

But if Noele was the undisputed Queen Bee of Crossroads, she wasn't a prima donna. She was always the first to welcome newcomers to the cast, shaking hands and booming at them 'Hello, I'm Noele Gordon', – as if they didn't know !

Nolly's pride and joy was her Rolls Royce – registration number NG10. When Tony Adams first joined the cast he was delighted when she asked him if he wanted to nip into town with her, assuming they'd be travelling in style. Imagine his horror when Nolly led him to the bus stop and made him sort through his change to make sure he'd got the right fare ! I often used to go into town with her on the bus but as Nolly loved her 'public' we never got much shopping done – the entire time was spent signing autographs.

Apart from Noele's sad departure, the other great loss of 1981 was the death of Roger Tonge. We had become firm friends. I was privileged to see the quiet, shy side of him – he wrote wonderful poetry which he never showed anyone – but he also had a great sense of fun. One spring morning in the late sixties, he was giving me a lift to the studios when he said, conversationally, 'It's a shame, isn't it ?'

'What is ?'

'Haven't you heard,' he said in surprise. 'They're taking Crossroads off.'

I could hardly believe it – but as Roger pointed out, we'd had a good run for our money and I decided to be philosophical. When we got to Broad Street I said, 'I won't mention anything to the others. Or do they know ?'

'I shouldn't think so,' said Roger. 'April Fool !'

A lot of people didn't like the character of Sandy or the way Roger played the part but he never let it bother him – he even had a T-shirt printed 'I'm Allergic To Criticism'. It was Roger who said of our critics they were to us what pigeons were to Nelson's Column – and that's still standing !

I was the first person Roger confided in back in the mid seventies when he'd been feeling low and ill for some time. He suddenly announced he'd got some strange lumps on the upper part of his chest. I was terribly worried because although Roger lived with his parents he wasn't the best person in the world at looking after himself. He'd arrive at the studios in the morning with his hair still wet from the shower, looking as if he'd just got out of bed – and he had. Noele tried to 'mother' him and for a while we had suspected he didn't eat properly, even thinking he might be anorexic. When he came back from the doctor and said, 'I've got Hodgkin's Disease,' I was almost relieved. At the back of my mind I'd thought he was going to say cancer. Of course Hodgkin's *is* a form of cancer but I think only Noele, being more worldly wise and experienced, realised that from the first. The terrible irony of our storyline which had put Roger in a wheelchair when he was fit and well, only to have him attacked by a disease which would really debilitate him was not lost on Jack and he

My favourite photograph of me and Roger – from my own collection.

made strenuous efforts to write around Roger's frequent absences for treatment at the Royal Marsden Hospital. It was awful, as with anyone you love, to watch his slow decline. He would come back after his treatment looking absolutely drained. About this time, I bought myself a duffel coat from the children's department of a big store in Birmingham. It was for a boy aged thirteen. I looked at Roger and said, 'You know, Rog, that'd fit you.' 'I think you're right,' he said and went off and bought himself one – that's how thin he'd become. You could see everything was a struggle but I still didn't think – or perhaps I refused to accept – that he was dying.

One day he turned up at the studios and said with a grin, 'I've got spots !' Somehow or other, he'd caught chicken pox. It was Ronnie Allen who said, 'Don't you think you ought to tell the Marsden ?' When he did, they insisted he went down there and into isolation. At the weekend he phoned me sounding quite chirpy, saying he was feeling better – but it was the last time I spoke to him. He died the next day, of heart failure – his system was so weak it could not cope with the infection. Poor Roger, he was only thirty-five and still looked about fifteen.

I read the lesson at his funeral but I still find it hard to believe he is dead and can feel his presence to this day. Of all the ghosts floating around the Central studios, I believe his is the most benign and friendly, just like the way he lived his life.

Romance in the Air

The path of true love never runs smoothly in soap opera and the Motel has been littered with broken hearts over the years.

Sandy, despite his disability, had a number of girlfriends and struck up an especially close relationship with secretary Faye Mansfield (Fiona Curzon).

David Hunter's track record isn't much better – he wanted to marry globe-trotting journalist Angela Kelly (Justine Lord) but she refused to be tied down and he had to settle for a quick cocktail with her between assignments.

(Opposite) Three years into his marriage to Barbara Brady he got involved with old flame, Sarah Alexander (Annette Andre) who became pregnant. Barbara stood by him and saved the marriage.

(Left) The devil and the deep blue sea . . . Debbie's true love is Deadly Dave (Breffni McKenna). He says he loves her . . . but did he just want an order for fifty multi-packs of frozen swede? And what about Maureen and the kids back in Spalding?

(Below left) Never mind . . . there's always childhood sweetheart Terry (Trevor Harrison). Their names are carved together on a bench at Dudley Zoo.

(Above) Love's young dream . . . or is it? There was a 'Do Not Disturb' notice permanently on the door of Chalet 7 when Daniel (Philip Goodhew) and Fiona (Caroline Evans) were having their fling, to the annoyance of Daniel's room-mate, Charlie Mycroft. But love foundered when Bomber gave Daniel the sack.

(Opposite) There was a time when Adam had to romance every pretty girl in sight, something which greatly upset Jill. Here he is in a moment of togetherness with Miranda Pollard (Claire Faulconbridge).

8
The Show Goes On

Tony Adams and I had great fun preparing for our screen wedding, including a visit to the sumptuous Janet Reger salon in London. Tony was most put out when Wardrobe bought me the satin negligée in the picture but couldn't afford his silk dressing gown.

(Opposite above) A solemn moment in church . . . David Hunter looks as if he's about to warn me off !

(Opposite below) Poised to cut the cake – though Sid Hooper looks as if he's seen a ghost. One of my previous husbands, perhaps ?

Roger had gone, Nolly had gone. It was unthinkable, but we carried on, in the hope that happier times were round the corner.

When the Jill/Adam romance had been on, off, on, off and on again it was decided the viewers wouldn't stand any more messing about and we were to be married. I was thrilled to bits because Tony Adams and I are great friends and if you've got to get married to someone on screen it does help if you like them ! The whole wedding thing was terrific fun from start to finish. Tony and I went to choose a ring, and to Janet Reger's salon in London to choose my honeymoon nightie, and then there was all the excitement of choosing the dress – not just for me but for Sorrel who, as Sarah Jane, was to be my bridesmaid. As she's never been a bridesmaid before or since, it was her big day. The wedding reception pictures were taken in the very grand surroundings of Hagley Hall, and to cap it all it was Jack's idea to bring Noele back for a reunion on our honeymoon in Venice. As usual, the affair was shrouded in secrecy and we all travelled separately so the papers would be thrown off the scent. None of us knew where we were going until only days before take-off and I was still acting dumb with reporters on the phone as the taxi to take me to the airport waited in the drive. I was thrilled to be going abroad with the programme, doubly so when I discovered we were travelling first class. 'Not too much champagne,' I warned Tony, 'we've got our lines to learn.' But he was much more interested in peering out of the window, craning his neck to see what the stewardesses were up to and trying to peek into the cabin. When questioned, he confessed – worldly, sophisticated Adam Chance had never been on a plane before in his life !

Venice was everything the brochures say and more but we didn't do much sightseeing – we were there three days and working all the time. It was August, height of the summer season and very, very hot. We had an enforced siesta when everything was closed in the middle of the day, so to make up the time we started at 8.00 in the morning and filmed till 8.00 at night.

One of the funniest times was when Tony and I had to climb up a bell tower to be used as a vantage point over the sights of Venice.

Venice, 'Bride of the Sea' – what more romantic place for a honeymoon ? We loved being ferried about in a gondola . . .

. . . but Tony and I discovered a mutual fear of heights on the bell tower above St Mark's Square, with Producer Jack Barton giving us directions with the aid of coloured handkerchiefs !

When we reached the top, after about a million spiral steps, it was no more than a sloping roof with a tiny, thin guard rail. Tony and I are both hopeless with heights and neither of us dared look down. Jack had got special permission to be on the roof of St Mark's and was going to radio directions across to us. So much for technology ! The

(Opposite) The highlight of Venice was the reunion with Meg, which Adam had organised as a surprise. This was the last time Nolly and I worked together.

walkie talkie broke down and he ended up issuing directions with coloured hankies. A white hankie meant to point in one direction, a red one meant stop and look in another. In this way Jill and Adam pointed out Venetian landmarks to the viewers. Tony and I couldn't wait to get down, but when we were finally finished, to our horror, we heard the clatter of feet on the stairs. The tourists had started arriving for the morning shift and were piling out on to this tiny space. We were being pushed closer and closer towards the edge . . . we finally made it down to terra firma and I've never been so grateful. Give me a studio scene and the set falling over any day of the week – I can cope with that !

Noele was involved in just two scenes and though they were very moving and were much appreciated by the viewers, there was something remote and strange about her which we could not understand. Now I believe it was the onset of her illness, which many people blame on the stress caused by the abruptness and surprise of her sacking. I am always sorry that this clouded the last time we worked together.

But there's a plus side to everything and as I no longer had my Mum in the programme I needed a close female friend to confide in – and found her in Diane. Sue Hanson and I had helped each other through various personal crises off the set and it was lovely to have her playing in the programme the role she fulfilled in real life. Sue is a warm, bubbly person and I think it's a shame that in later years the character of Diane didn't somehow develop and mature in the way it should. Sue also worked very closely with Sandor Eles, the charming Hungarian actor who played temperamental restaurant manager, Paul Ross. The Motel management also changed about this time with the arrival of the Pollards – J. Henry, Valerie and Miranda, played by Michael Turner, Heather Chasen and Claire Faulconbridge. As both Heather and Claire have beautiful auburn hair, we once again had a redhead involved in the running of the Motel ! On the other side of the studio floor was the garage and another collection of characters – Joe MacDonald (Carl Andrews), Jim Baines (John Forgeham) and Sid Hooper (Stan Stennett) – not forgetting sexy Sharon Metcalfe, played by Carolyn Jones.

There was a lot of fuss made about the year 1984 because of the title of George Orwell's book, and for 'Crossroads' it was to prove an ominous time. After the excitement of Venice things had settled down again and it was not until the summer break that I got the first rumblings that Something Was Going To Happen. Jack rang and asked if I'd go to a photocall at Cheltenham, where a lot of the exteriors were then filmed. I was a bit put out as I was supposed to be on holiday, but agreed. We did the photos, then Jack asked if he could put something in the back of my car. It was the two pastel drawings, supposedly of myself and Sandy as children, that had hung in Meg's sitting room. I had a funny feeling then that change was in the air, and it wasn't long before the nature of that change became known.

Her colleagues at the garage saw another side to sexy Sharon Metcalfe (above) when she befriended Nina (below), a little girl with Downs' syndrome. Sharon later quit her job as garage manageress to work with the mentally handicapped.

The off-stage dramas were set to overtake those on-stage but the programme still had some happy events to celebrate – like the christening of miracle baby Katy-Louise Banks (Emily Albu), here seen with proud parents Kevin and Glenda. Emily is Lynette's real-life daughter.

CROSSROADS 4000th Episode

On 2 November 1984, 'Crossroads' celebrated its 20th birthday and at the end of that month passed another milestone – the 4,000th episode. There were the usual photocalls, parties, speeches and people getting sloshed, but privately we thought it was rather odd. Surely the birthday to celebrate was the programme's 21st – and you didn't have to be of an unduly pessimistic nature to start thinking: 'Perhaps they're trying to tell us something. Perhaps we're not going to be around next year !' It was in this spirit that I organised my own party for the 20th anniversary, before it was too late ! Sure enough, a change did come, and it was announced that Jack Barton was leaving after seventeen years, to be replaced by Phillip Bowman. It felt like the end of an era.

Sunny smiles from the cast – in November, 1984 we celebrated our 20th anniversary and the 4,000th episode. But we were about to weather another storm with Producer Jack Barton making way for Phillip Bowman after 17 years.

Phillip had a very difficult task to do. In television terms, 'Crossroads' had to be dragged kicking and screaming not into the eighties but into the sixties. All other TV dramas – and that includes soaps – had a vastly different way of working. They were not cooped up in studio sets but did a lot more expensive location filming which gave a very realistic feel. This location filming was done close to transmission so there was some semblance of normality in seasons of the year. They had masses of editing time so that the best possible results were seen on screen. Above all, they recorded episodes out of order, rehearsing then recording all the scenes appropriate to one set before moving on to another. Phillip had to accomplish all these things for 'Crossroads' as well as follow his brief which was to make the programme more glamorous in the 'Dallas/Dynasty' mould. His answer to this was to bring in Gabrielle Drake as Nicola Freeman and make the Motel part of a huge chain of hotels of which her late husband had been Chairman. We all loved Gabrielle and she very quickly fitted into the studio routine and knuckled down to the discipline. She even put up with being mercilessly teased by Tony Adams, who called her 'Dora Duck' because of her name.

Tony has always joked that he reads *The Sun* to find out what's going on in the programme and for ages there had been rumours that there were going to be sackings among the cast. Pessimistic as ever I was convinced it was me and I was literally speechless when Ronnie Allen told me he and Sue had been to tea with Phillip at Brown's Hotel – and were to be axed from the show. It's to Ronnie's (and Gabrielle's) undying credit that in the month that they overlapped there was never any bitterness between them. Ronnie, as ever, was the perfect gentleman, and the saddest part was that in those last few months he gave some of his best performances – perhaps because he was more relaxed. I was also desperately sorry to see Sue go. We had had so many funny times together, and she was a lady who really had style. It was Sue who taught me about lighting, a legacy from all the films she'd been in. She pointed out to me which was the key light to step into – from there, all the rest followed. If I look younger on

Actors Philip Goodhew and Harry Nurmi in holiday mood at exotic Bradford Street, Birmingham.

screen today than I did when I started out twenty-three years ago, it's thanks to Sue and clever lighting, not some secret elixir of youth !

In December 1984 we had a very grand dinner attended by all the cast and production team which was a formal farewell to Jack. It was a sentimental sort of occasion, and we all autographed each other's menus. There were speeches and not a few tears shed. Nolly was there, looking very thin. A few weeks later, I called round with her Christmas present and was relieved to see her looking better. But it was a temporary remission and she died the following April. It was almost as if she was bowing out to make way for Gabrielle and we knew that at 'Crossroads' we had turned another page in the ledger and were about to begin again. The biggest irony of all was that, had Noele's illness not got worse, Phillip Bowman had wanted her back at the Motel.

Phillip, in short, changed everything. He changed the way the programme was recorded for the first time since we began. We were delighted that at last some money and resources were being directed at 'Crossroads' but it made long studio days even longer, with make-up calls an hour before you were needed, and as I always got the short

Nicola Freeman (Gabrielle Drake) arrived to take charge of the motel – but her private life always aroused more interest among the staff than her management methods – a rumoured affair with Lord Wilminster, marriage to Herbie Freeman and, finally, the appearance of her illegitimate daughter.

(Opposite) As Jill, I thought I'd found true love with Mickey Doyle. But Mickey saw true happiness only at the bottom of a whisky glass.

straw (I'm one of those people who never wins a raffle), I was at the studio early in the morning and inevitably in the last scene at night. Phillip also organised our move to bigger rehearsal rooms in Bradford Street and found us some new locations at Penns Hall Hotel, Sutton Coldfield, for motel exteriors and a leisure centre near Birmingham. All location filming really means is standing about for hours in the freezing cold or wet or both, and we got very cunning at rolling up our long johns under summer dresses and cutting the necks out of thermal vests so they didn't show with low-cut tops. I soon got wise to working on location and once the master shot had shown me gaily tripping out of the Motel in my court shoes in November, it was on with the furry boots for the rest of the scene !

As with any changes there were teething troubles. The logistics were overwhelming. The call sheets for the cast and the crewing requirements on the technical side were vastly complicated. I was so used to the old routine, rigid as it was, that I felt a lot of time was spent running twice the distance to make one step forward. Everything took so long. In the old days, probably because Jack and Reg were

(Opposite) The 'coming-of-age' I thought we wouldn't see – 'Crossroads' 21st anniversary in November, 1985. Left to right: Pamela Vezey, (Kath), Steven Pinder (Roy), Paul Henry (Benny), Dorothy Brown (Lorraine), Sue Hanson (Diane), Tony Adams (Adam), Harry Nurmi (Barry), Philip Goodhew (Daniel), Carl Andrews ('Mac'), Dee Hepburn (Ann-Marie), Patrick Jordan (Darby).

Adam was thrilled when he had to compere the 'Miss Crossroads' competition. It was won by Receptionist Ann-Marie Wade (Dee Hepburn).

more experienced, decisions were taken much faster, and because we all knew each other and got along so well, we used a sort of shorthand so things weren't endlessly discussed. Now there was a lot of consultation (some of it fruitful) but there was also a lot of time and energy spent on things that, to me, didn't really matter.

But Phillip did work some mini-miracles. For the first time we had the real security of monthly or six-monthly contracts. The money perked up. We had a proper wardrobe allowance. And there were some lovely additions to the cast. Phillip Goodhew, a real heart-breaker, joined as Nicola's spoilt stepson, Daniel. There was Mary Lincoln as his sister Joanna, bubbly Dee Hepburn as Anne-Marie from Scotland, Steve Pinder as her love interest, and Patrick Jordan as Darby. I fully expected Jill to merge into the background and was flattered, if rather surprised, when Phillip told me he saw Jill as a very feminine, sexy person and he had a big love story in mind! Mickey Doyle (Martin Smith) became Kings Oak's answer to Sylvester Stallone when he grabbed Jill from under Adam's nose and this led into a very serious story as Mickey's drinking got progressively worse and nearly dragged Jill down with him.

In November 1985, contrary to my predictions, we did 'come of age' with our 21st birthday and I wondered again if there could be life after Nolly. But just when things seemed to be settling down there came another bombshell. Phillip was leaving, to be replaced by the man the papers were to call 'Butcher Bill' – William Smethurst.

Producer William Smethurst – the man the papers called 'Butcher Bill'.

Moving with the Times

Lisa Lancaster (Alison Dowling), 'Bomber' Lancaster's younger daughter, on the phone to one of her many lovers back in Rome ! At Christmas 1987 she brought one of them – Giorgio – back to meet the family.

*I*f Stone Age Man had been hooked on soap operas, instead of tuning in to 'Crossroads' or 'Kings Oak' he would have watched a programme called 'Slohtran Ford' because, so the village guidebook (originally sold in the Post Office in Miss Tatum's day for 1/6d), tells us, that was the original name for the village. Meaning 'marshy ford', the hamlet was originally inhabited by foresters who built their huts at the easiest fording or crossing point of the River Slotter. At least, that's what we were told when the programme was devised !

The name Kings Oak comes from the Civil War when, as Tommy Lancaster was delighted to discover, King Charles hid there for a night in a giant oak tree - which may or may not be the very one still standing on the right of the drive at the hotel. But as Tommy would be the first to admit, it hardly matters, as long as on special occasions he can persuade the staff to dress up in wench costumes in the Merry Monarch Bar . . .

In 1969, the writers' 'Bible' established that the village of Kings Oak had 750 inhabitants and was administered by its own Rural District Council. It had a police house, the 'Rivoli' cinema and a railway station (both, sadly, now closed), as well as two churches, St Lawrence's Church of England and the Methodist Chapel, and three pubs – the Crown, the King's Oak and the Running Stag. The only one we visit today is the Stag, recently taken over by John Maddingham and his errant wife Eve. The Kings Oak Stores, the village grocery, was modernised and reopened in 1986 and is run by Margaret Grice with a little help and a lot of hindrance from her family, Ray, Beverley and Jason, and her interfering mother, Mrs Babbitt.

The Motel guidebook is more specific about the origins of 'Crossroads' itself. The Motel was opened on 17 April 1963 by Meg Richardson, née Fraser, widow of Charles Richardson, a talented landscape artist who worked as a cartoonist for the *Birmingham Post*. On his death she turned her family home into a motel by building eighteen chalets in the grounds.

In 1969 a room cost £2 15s 0d a night (payable in advance), and a drink at the bar (then situated in Reception), would cost between 1/8d for a lowly bottle of brown ale to 5/6d for an exotic 'vodka and tomato juice' – no cocktail 'Happy Hour' then, and certainly no mention of a 'Bloody Mary' ! A fashionable gin and orange or gin and lime would set you back just 3/4d. The bar closed at 10.30 pm but residents could get a drink after hours from a separate stock.

Charlie Mycroft and Darby in the reception of the new 'Kings Oak Country Hotel'.

(Below) A new landlord for the 'Running Stag' – Jeremy Nicholas joined the company to play John Maddingham, and Christopher Duffy plays his son Jamie.

The Motel has been refurbished four times, twice from necessity – in 1967 when workmen accidentally exploded a wartime bomb and in 1981 when it was destroyed by fire – and twice from choice. Nicola Freeman's interior designer 'BB' revamped it in 1985 but when Tommy Lancaster took over he decided it was time for a move up market and 'Crossroads' became 'Kings Oak Country Hotel' complete with oak panelling, flame-stitch footstools, and the Merry Monarch Bar.

(Above left) The Grice Family – hated by many viewers but considered the 'best part of the programme' by many others. Jason (Simon Lowe), Beverley (Karen Murden), Ray (Al Ashton), and Margaret (Meryl Hampton).

10

The Final Chapter

Tommy 'Bomber' Lancaster (Terence Rigby) owner of the Red Ox steakhouse chain, took over Crossroads Motel in January 1987.

On 10 June 1987 the cast and production team were invited to a buffet party given by Central Television's Director of Programmes, Andy Allan. The Controller of Drama, Ted Childs, was there, and so was the new Managing Director, Leslie Hill. It was a very jolly evening and spirits were high. 'Crossroads' had undergone some remarkable changes since William Smethurst took over as producer but everything seemed to be coming together very happily. The scripts were getting better and better, with some lovely comedy scenes as the new writers settled down. For my part, I was enjoying playing Jill Chance more than I had for a long time.

The new members of cast, too, were settling down – and what a lot of them there were ! The changes had been so dramatic that Andy Allan's party was the first opportunity many of us had to meet each other socially.

I had been delighted when Terence Rigby joined us in November 1986 to play the abrasive but warm-hearted 'Bomber' Lancaster. He set the standard for some splendid acting talent to join the company. First Graham Seed (better known then as Nigel Pargetter from 'The Archers') as the duffer Charlie Mycroft, and then Elsie Kelly as the charlady Mrs Tardebigge (a character so disliked she was written out only to soar in popularity so much she had to be quickly written in again !). After that the changes came thick and fast. Caroline Evans as Fiona Harding, and Glyn Pritchard as the young assistant Chef arrived, and no sooner had they settled in than we were welcoming Katherine Hurlbutt as Debbie and saying 'hello' to the entire 'Grice' family – Meryl Hampton as Margaret, Al Ashton as Ray, Karen Murden (sixteen years old and in her first big role) as Beverley, and Birmingham schoolboy Simon Lowe as Jason.

Both Karen and Simon rapidly became teenage 'cult' figures – sometimes with unfortunate results. On one occasion poor Simon was mobbed by girl fans on a bus and the driver threw him off !

By June we had been joined by Tara Shaw as Tara the sports instructor (and lover for Adam !), Shona Lindsay as Sara, and Ashok Kumar as Beverley's boyfriend Ranjit.

(Above) Fiona Harding whose daddy owns a chicken farm (famous for its butterbreast chickens) and mummy owns a chihuahua.

(Right) A thoughtful Tara . . . her social-worker boyfriend Robin has found out that she is 'having it off with Old Smoothie-chops' Adam Chance !

We were all in buoyant mood and so, apparently, was Central Television. Important developments were in the offing ! An hour-long omnibus was planned for Sunday lunchtime viewing in the Midlands, and a new titles sequence was being developed to replace the pictures of the red MG Maestro on its endless trip to the Motel. The City of Birmingham Symphony Orchestra was recording new music with top saxophonist Raf Ravenscroft of Pink Floyd fame, and, most dramatic of all, the name 'Crossroads' was to be dropped from the beginning of September and we were going to be called 'Kings Oak'.

It was all very exciting, and William did not try to hide his relief that things were working out well. He had been brought in from the BBC with the brief to shake 'Crossroads' up and he had done it with unusual thoroughness. All the writers of six months ago had gone, we had two new script editors (Diane Culverhouse and Veronica Henry, also from the BBC), and the cast had almost completely changed. We were used to being 'shaken-up' by people ordered to drag us into the seventies, or eighties, or 21st century or whatever, but nobody had changed things quite as radically as this !

There had, admittedly, been some dodgy moments, with writers who were still feeling their way, and members of cast who were settling in. But by the evening of Andy Allan's party everything was beginning to work. We were brimming with confidence and when we heard about the weekend omnibus it seemed the best news possible. I felt sure an omnibus would introduce the programme to a whole new set of viewers – people not normally home to watch television at 6.35 p.m. in the evening; people who thought 'Crossroads' was rubbish without ever having watched it; people who might have watched it years ago but had lost the habit. The programme was good enough, we felt sure, to win them back.

During the next three weeks our confidence continued to grow. In the studio we recorded episodes by our new writers Margaret Phelan, Helen Leadbeater, and Andy Rashleigh, which would be transmitted in late August and early September, the time of the great change from 'Crossroads' to 'Kings Oak'. On 19 June the CBSO came in to the Central music studio to record our new music. In the production office, William, Michele Buck (our super-efficient and very bubbly associate producer), and designer Stuart Kettle were poring over still photographs of the Warwickshire countryside, specially commissioned for our new titles sequence. Every time Tony Adams or I went near the office we were dragged in to listen to the new music and give our opinion on the pictures that would best go with it.

Even more cheering, the programme was rapidly picking up in the ratings. Despite the most massive changes in cast ever experienced by a soap opera in Britain we were regularly getting two episodes out of three in the ITV top ten, and the ratings on 26 June showed us at number four. That week, only three other programmes on the entire ITV network had proved more popular than we were !

On that last weekend in June two meetings of vital importance to 'Crossroads' were held in country hotels. One meeting we knew about. It was the regular script conference, held monthly at the Elms Country Hotel, Abberley in Worcestershire. These script conferences always started on a Sunday afternoon, continued through dinner (a rather splendid dinner, we members of cast suspected, although the script editors always claimed they were working too hard to notice), and then resumed next morning.

During the two-day meetings storylines would be plotted for the next four weeks of scripts. Sitting round a conference table (or sipping cognac after dinner !), the writers and script editors would decide on whether our characters should be happy or sad, good or bad, sympathetic or unsympathetic, do believable things or ridiculous things – decide, in fact, whether our characters should live or die !

But on that last weekend in June, while William and his team pondered on our individual futures, another meeting was pondering the future for all of us. It was a meeting of top ITV executives, and while the 'Crossroads' team decided on our stories for the winter, the ITV executives were told by Andy Allen that 'Crossroads' was to be axed.

William was still at the script conference at Abberley when Ted Childs phoned and gave him the news. He spoke about it privately to Michele then carried on with the meeting as if nothing had happened. 'Except that we all *knew* something had happened,' one of the script editors told me, 'You could sense it. At lunchtime William cut the meeting short and disappeared off with Michele. The rest of us sat on the lawn, ate a chocolate roulade, drank a bottle of wine, and wondered what we would do next. We simply *knew* it was all up.'

The script editors were told officially the next evening, and it was decided to tell the cast after the studio finished on the Thursday.

Before then there was a minor panic when the *Daily Mirror* discovered what was happening, having been tipped-off by a waitress who overheard a discussion in a restaurant ! The *Mirror* did not use the story, however, and when the cast were called together by William and Ted and told that 'Crossroads' was to end, the news came as a total shock.

I was not at the meeting. I had finished in the studio in the afternoon and gone home. William phoned me a few minutes before the general announcement was made. 'Are you sitting down ?' he asked. 'Do I need to be ?' I replied. 'Yes,' said William, and told me that the job I had so enjoyed doing for the past twenty-three years was over. . . .

'Why ?' we all asked, 'why when the programme is still so popular, and when so many good writers and talented actors have just been brought in – some actors not yet seen on the screen ! – is the programme being killed ?' There was bitterness at first, and a sense of betrayal. It is easy to say that twenty-three years is a good run for any programme – but not easy to accept when you are actually being 'chopped'.

The funeral of Mary Lancaster brought two new characters into the programme. Lisa Lancaster, who flew home from Rome, and Terry Butterworth, an old family friend from Dudley.

Darby has a stern word with Mrs Tardebigge (Elsie Kelly), who has been up to no good with her feather duster.

William told me the programme was in an impossible situation. New, younger middle-class viewers would not watch 'Crossroads' because of our image, but our older, traditional viewers were bitterly upset by any attempt to change things. Central felt they had given him as long as they could to do an impossible job.

Well, I thought they should have given us all longer – and so, it seemed, did many of our viewers. Almost immediately, the letters started pouring in:

'It seems a bit daft to kill off "Crossroads" just when it is getting so much better. There will, I am sure, be many regular viewers like myself who will otherwise suffer severe withdrawal symptoms . . .'

'I must say the characters of recent times have become more believable and sincere, especially in the last year . . . is there any hope of a re-consideration ? It is a harmless, gentle programme . . .'

'Please don't make all the millions of viewers who enjoy the show just now suffer at the expense of those who mock. Nobody forces them to tune in. For once, take notice of everyone who watches and enjoys Crossroads every week . . .'

Beverley Grice and her friend Sara Briggs (Shona Lindsay) discuss their skiing holiday in the bar of The Running Stag – but what is producer William Smethurst doing in the background ?

Mrs Babbitt (Margaret Stallard) checks on the price of biscuits and worries about her savings in the Bradford and Bingley. Her son-in-law Ray wants £5000 to start a taxi business – but will he really run her home every night in a white Rolls Royce ?

'I and all of my family love the show. Since Tommy, Charles, Debbie and the Grice family have come into it it's been great fun . . .'

'Although I liked Mrs Freeman and staff I really like the new "Boss" and family and staff even more. PLEASE PLEASE cannot the decision to close be reversed ?'

'I wrote several weeks ago to tell you how happy I was with the changes made in "Crossroads", only to find a few days later the powers that be had decided to axe the series ! All the best for the future. Sorry to see you go.'

And we're sorry to say goodbye !

(Opposite) 'You won't recognise this place by the time I've finished with it', a determined Tommy Lancaster tells the new General Manager, Jill.